EXCERPTS
from
the
REAL WORLD

# Excerpts from the Real World

*a prose poem in ten parts*

## ROBERT KROETSCH

1986

oolichan books

Lantzville, British Columbia

Canadian Cataloguing in Publication Data

Kroetsch, Robert, 1927-
  Excerpts from the real world

    ISBN 0-88982-063-5 (limited ed.).
    ISBN 0-88982-059-7 (pbk)

    I. Title.
PS8521.R64E9 1986      C811'.54      C86-091302-3
PR9199.3.K76E9 1986

Publication of this book has been financially assisted by the
Canada Council.

Published by
OOLICHAN BOOKS
Box 10, Lantzville, B.C. V0R 2H0

Printed in Canada by
MORRISS PRINTING COMPANY LTD.
Victoria, British Columbia

*for*
*George Bowering*
*and*
*Ron Smith*

*and for you,*
*Ishtar*

# Acknowledgements

Sections of this poem, in various forms, have appeared in *Dandelion, NeWest Review, Border Crossings, Canadian Literature, Whetstone, True North/Down Under, Rubicon, Lines Review* (Scotland) and *Poetry Australia*. I am grateful to their editors.

The author is grateful to Ian Garrioch for the use of his fine painting, *Ascents of Perspective*.

"Perhaps if I call you forever
	you'll hear me toward the end."

—from *The Missing Book of Cucumbers*

*Being an*
*Introduction*
*to Strawberries*
*and Cream*

## 7/1/85

I want to explain why I didn't answer the door. I knew it was you, there. My reason for not answering was very simple at the time, though now it seems more complex. It was late morning on a January day. The sun was shining blatantly.

## 11/1/85

You say that in your view everything is poetry. Then you go skiing with your mother while I spend the afternoon trying to put the scales back onto the fish.

## 12/1/85

Early one evening in Rome I bought four blood oranges from a street vendor and went to my hotel room and cut each of the four oranges in half and sat alone in my room, studying the color of blood oranges, listening to the rain.

### 14/1/85

I couldn't wear the belt you bought me to the dinner you cooked for us in your apartment. I was wearing socks that didn't match. Your telephone was un-plugged. CBC hadn't broadcast its quota of Beet-hoven for the day. The scallops were drowned in a wine sauce that tasted of your eyes.

### 23/1/85

So one of us is the jealous lover. The photograph you sent me, of a strawberry on a fishhook. Thank you. I just want to explain why I sent it to you. Anonymously, of course. How did you know it was from me?

### 30/1/85

I have spent the entire store of my pain. My life is a portrait of the woman who deceived me into hunt-ing the unicorn.

The original plan was to build a pyramid on the sand dunes of southwestern Manitoba. Blue apricots are rare. Perhaps the apricots are plums. Doors, in a manner of speaking, are descriptive. Otherwise we wouldn't be here now.

I should not have sought the unicorn beside the sea. Your long hair spills down your back, before we make love, like seaweed in the Bay of Fundy. When you make love. Like the Bay of Fundy.

Each entry, by its coming into existence, excludes itself from the potential of the poem. The spending lover both creates and fears the growing silence. Annihilation.

## 14/2/85

About the night we danced in the kitchen, drunk on the wine that the scallops did not drink. The socks you were wearing, you said, were your mother's. What if, for instance, we replaced the unicorn with the common mallard or the garter snake?

## 15/2/85

You say that, as a child, you liked playing hide and seek. Of the three roses I sent you, one was touched by frost. We fall through the gaps in your words. The net, too, is a container of sorts.

## 16/2/85

I want to explain. Words surface from inside, bringing with them vinegar and whales. Your eyes grow darker when you eat figs or when you flirt with other men. Owls pick up mice. Sky burial, you might call it.

## 18/2/85

Once, years ago, I was in Mexico and got sick on some lettuce I ate in a small village. Figs, on the other hand, appropriate the shade of blue that most imitates desire.

## 20/2/85

In the switchblade of your tongue, the fish hawk studies mayhem. Tell me again that you love me. Which of the three roses did you put into the spaghetti?

## 23/2/85

Ask your friend, the mounted policeman, to read Lacan. Identity, he should realize, is at once impossible and unavoidable. Desire is that which stands outside the boundaries of satisfaction.

## 24/2/85

*L'autre.* The author. I'm not myself today. The other is a tramp. Confloozied.

## 25/2/85

In hopscotch, you may recall, the pieces of broken glass kiss the pavement as a beginning. And snow turns the wide world into an egg.

## 26/2/85

Lapwing is, improbably, the name of a bird. Titmouse. Goatsucker.

## 27/2/85

Our lunch in Niverville. The seed-cleaning plants were shaking the sky. You listed your truckdriver-lovers, on the paper plate, under my fish and chips. The man at the next table passed us the catsup.

## 28/2/85

We are on the appropriate flyway. I have not seen a single ibis in years. The flight of butterflies, from your pubic hair, came to my nose as a metaphysical proposition. For a moment I believed in paradise.

*Telegram,*
*or,*
*Tell Your*
*Grandma*

## 1/3/85

I did not intend to enter the story. It happened by accident, believe me. You were wearing sunglasses.

## 2/3/85

The affair I never mention, the one that turns out to be with you, was occasioned by an ice storm that toppled power lines and brought angels crashing into the frozen fields.

## 4/3/85

Telescopes are aphrodisiacs. The kiss you gave me last night was a comet from a galaxy which is, I now read in the almanac of your body, undiscoverable. Trucks loaded with sugar beets roar past my apartment at four in the morning.

## 5/3/85

Just before sunrise, I drink the juice of four blood oranges. So one of us is the jealous lover. If strawberries grew in snow, they'd be easier to find at night. I miss the smell of your hair.

## 8/3/85

I want to explain why I like the country & western songs you compose in your sleep. She's a cheatin lyin woman/with a cheatin lyin song./She's a cheatin lyin woman,/so I know we'll get along.

## 10/3/85

That role of barbed wire you put in my bed. Don't you realize I could have hurt myself, mistaking it for you?

## 13/3/85

Horsehair, when mixed with plaster, contributes to the durability of the wall. And, O yes, did I mention that the quality I dislike most about you is your absence? Apples are improved by the first frost. The memory is a careless optician.

## 14/3/85

I hadn't noticed the margin. Eli Mandel was lectur-
ing on the myth of the frontier, this on the banks of
the Oldman River, to a band of Blackfoot warriors. I
fell off the page. The sun, unthinkingly (or so we
assume), bruised itself red on the flat horizon.

## 15/3/85

I liked the telegram, the one you sent me reporting
my birth. And the bouquet of thistles, that too
bespoke a generosity and a thoughtfulness I hadn't
anticipated. But why did you have the florist send
me the bill in a black envelope?

## 16/3/85

She was drinking straight tequila,/she was having
lots of fun./She was laughing like a raven,/she was
carrying a gun.

## 17/3/85

Yours are the unicorn's buttocks. I recognized that,
the first time you knelt to my whisper. But how do I
capture you, ever?

## 18/3/85

The silence of the pickerel fills Lake Winnipeg. The lake is shallow. We are building a pyramid in the middle of the lake. Once, years ago, watching a flock of ducks feeding in a slough, I fired my 12-gauge shotgun into a passing rainbow.


## 19/3/85

Would it not be safer for me to say, in addressing you, *Red* roses are red?


## 20/3/85

To live a long life. To help others. To have fun. These, the old hunter explained, are the Inuit values. This was in Eskimo Point, on Hudson Bay. A polar bear, hunting a hunter, the old hunter explained, approaches the way a cat approaches. Or something like that. He was trying to make Terry understand. My friend Terry Heath, years ago, before he visited Eskimo Point, was a collector of art.

22/3/85

Nothing pleases a perfect wife, nothing. I told that
to the blizzard. The blizzard shrieked with laughter.
Since then I've travelled often to strange places,
rain forests and tropical islands. I'm planning a
collection of turtle eggs.

23/3/85

Don Kerr invented Saskatoon by growing up inside
a downtown movie palace. He refuses to record the
prairie wind. Now, today, he asks for a section of
my poem for *NeWest Review*. I've applied to the
Canada Council for a pair of running shoes and a
whistle.

24/3/85

Your nipples are the color of pennies, found in the
snow. I am a stranger's hand. Even our secrecy is
become a form of devotion.

This is a poem I didn't write. And not because I wasn't writing. And not because it isn't a poem. I'm beside myself, purely as a way to anticipate the past. Endings have stems and blossoms.

*On the*
    *Uncertainty*
*of the Singer's*
        *Lamentable*
*(_____)*

**1/4/85**

I only buy used mirrors now. I like to see other faces when I look at myself.


**2/4/85**

If it is true, as you sometimes insist, that I cannot bear to be loved, why, then, do you, so often, transform yourself into a distant city?


**3/4/85**

Here on the coast of North Dakota, we pretend against our desire. Over wine and chilled oysters, we touch each other with promises. In the seaweed on the shore of your bed, we smell the cold film of our spent bodies. Which of us wrote the narrative line?


**4/4/85**

Your body is so smooth when you sleep, lobsters, moving along the ocean floor, bruise the water to a rougher sheen. On damp nights especially, my tongue hides under your pubic hairs. We must be sensible.

7/4/85

I'm delighted that you went to communion this morning. Angels, with the loss of their natural habitat, are becoming scarcer. I'm happy to be able to regret that I met you.


8/4/85

You are what used to be called a sharp-tongued woman. Look what you've gone and done to my pricked rejoinder.


9/4/85

In my imagination, this morning, rabbits, coming wet out of the sea, eat your shadow.


10/4/85

Today I'm having an affair with a wine pitcher I bought, years ago, in Sienna, and accidentally left behind in the Leonardo da Vinci Airport, outside Rome. The radio in the kitchen is paralyzed by my infidelity.

### 11/4/85

"But most of all I luv you cuz yr you." If you see what I mean.


### 12/4/85

I remembered you, for four days, with my broken skin. We live our lives expecting phone calls. You dingaling.


### 14/4/85

Here in the Highlands the budded trees, obscenely mauve, ache to blossom. How do man and woman, in these blocky houses, speak against such arrays of stone? Thinking of you, I forgot to pack a sweater. Tell your new lover to wear glass pyjamas when he sets out from Winnipeg to transport bull semen around the world.

15/4/85

You are so far distant, I eat black pudding to keep
my anger from turning to dismay. Unexpectedly, I
see that expectancy is what draws us to the clouds,
the clouds to us. Last night, late, the trees outside
my window were holding hands. I miss you, apparently.


17/4/85

When we wear wool, we wear grass. The carnivor-
ous earth awaits my version of reciprocity. Inter-
twined universes inhabit each of our bodies.


18/4/85

Is the terrible the part we know or the part we
don't? Why is it so difficult to grow apples in the
dark, without having them turn into potatoes?
How did the Atlantic, so dryly, assert itself between
us? Did you remember to pay my hydro bill?

19/4/85

My beard needs shaping. The sun has been gone for a week. Is it possible that, for the split fraction of a second, I saw the hole in the window before the bullet pierced my skull?

20/4/85

But most of all I love you. The rabbits have no shadows of their own. The mirror falls into its own error.

21/4/85

Peter Easingwood quotes John Cowper Powys to me. "I like a chaotic anarchistic strung-along *multi-verse*..."

22/4/85

Headline in the Dundee newspaper: Corpse Found in Graveyard. To lock is to key. Even as I lay down, I heard myself walking away.

It was fourteen long days to the moonlight. I have
won, I have won, cried the raven.

*Every*
*Idea Is*
*a Wish*

24/4/85

You live an unsigned life. Like the ashtray I bought in Edinburgh (the castle, the castle), you remind me of where I once was. Kitschy-kitschy-coo, love. And I don't even smoke. Do I?

25/4/85

Hammer Happy, the King of Babylon, sells used cars on the Pembina strip, right there in Winnipeg. Even here, now, today, this afternoon in the Yorkshire Dales, I locate my pain in the descending lines of a prairie coulee. Your heart breaks me.

26/4/85

Everything recurs (more or less). Consider, for instance, spring. Or transmission problems.

28/4/85

And so she tracked you down. You, the Shyster King of Babble On, she, with her friend Pontiac, the old chief disguised as a red coupe with mags on the rear and a four-barreled carburetor. The three of you making it, together. Kinky.

30/4/85

"Stay gentle passenger & reade A sentence sent thee from ye dead." This I found on a church wall, in York. Ron Smith and I were shopping for Harris Tweed jackets.

2/5/85

I go through the secondhand bookstores of Amsterdam, looking for a single remaining copy of my first book, the book I never wrote. It was a study of the silence of cucumbers.

3/5/85

Trying to prove that Western Canada is inscribed in Hammer Happy's six-month warranty, I watch for magpies (dancing) in the tulip fields. I try to snare gophers with a fishing line, here, below sea level.

5/5/85

Rijksmuseum. "Wild man on a unicorn with a bird. Engraving, c. 1450. From the large deck of playing cards." Self portrait with still life. Consider, for instance, the stealth of the cucumber.

6/5/85

I want to explain why I mailed you that team of horses for your birthday. I know you have nowhere to keep them. Except in your mother's garage.

8/5/85

There, outside the restaurant, near the tram stop, chalked on a small blackboard: TOMAATEN EN KOMKOMMER. Every clue is, surely, a clue. *Broodje*, I tell myself, clutching at straws, must be sandwich. Bread, as a root word, belatedly, perhaps.

9/5/85

Desire, like a prairie duck, its tail feathers in the air, feeds below the surface. As Hammer Happy would have it: poet, consider shock absorbers. They are not ashamed to repeat themselves. Relax, and you'll kitsch yourself laughing.

11/5/85

And yet I felt a certain twinge of disappointment when we were told the plane was about to crash. I had intended to invest in RRSPs.

### 14/5/85

STASIS. Bus stop. The Greeks have a knack for starring. The unsigned hole in the universe. Not to mention the street vendors, their carts, at this time of year, heaped with strawberries. Passengers.

### 25/5/85

Here on Mandraki Beach, Skiathos, I undress. The wind makes of each of your nipples a cork, of my mouth a bottle that begs a signature.

### 27/5/85

Tsougria (Thistle) Island is presently (since The War, I'm told) uninhabited. I squat naked beside the stone slabs of the abandoned olive-crushing floor. I grunt and then sigh. Ah, life, I think, watching the butterflies and the lizards. I tear in half the Kleenex snitched from your beach bag. These are the economies of islands.

Slices of fresh cucumber, with just a drop of vinegar, a drab of salt. Pass me that ashtray. Let place do the signing for us. Close the door and let me in.

*The Frying Pan,
and How
It Was Actually
Invented*

## 7|6|85

We're on the road to Lake Winnipeg. The pelicans are measuring the sky for a new suit of clouds. The gophers measure the width of the road with their lives. You put your left hand on my right thigh. Floor it, you say.

## 8|6|85

Two loves halve I, you wrote on your last postcard, the one you sent from Riding Mountain. You are as beautiful as snow. I'm sorry the hill fell off your skis.

## 11|6|85

They boarded up the railway station while I was inside, waiting for the last train to nowhere. Later the same day I heard the waters of the lake beginning to rise. Someone offered me an iron raft. Thank you.

## 14|6|85

Love is a frying pan with a handle that conducts heat.

## 16/6/85

The sky takes on the color of what you and I, mistakenly I'm told, call the crocus. Why don't we, then, by way of recompense to both Nature and Language, find a small bluff of poplars and have a slow quickie?

## 17/6/85

I had no idea that, in a previous incarnation, you were a Spanish guitarist. With a minimum of one finger, you are able to play the music of your passionate recollection. I have come especially to like the smell of your right hand.

## 18/6/85

"Harlequin Presents" Number 426. "Then he led her into the forward cabin and gently laid her on the made-up berth, her fair hair falling across the pillows. For a moment he sat on the edge of the bunk, his eyes dark with desire as he fondled her." And besides, we were in a rowboat.

19/6/85

Praxis makes perfect, you tell me. But I'm Dedalus on my feet.

20/6/85

Gimli Proverb. And I'll tellya another thing, young lady. If I hadn't spent so much money on sex and booze, I'd have more money now to spend on sex and booze.

25/6/85

We've been promised a weather of grasshoppers, yet nothing hatches. When will you leave your retailer of bull semen, there on the outskirts of Brandon, and buy a ticket to the Equator? In your absence I practice sleeping in the middle of the bed.

28/6/85

And I suppose, dear, you think I have never got one of your pubic hairs stuck in *my* throat. Gates are inclined to swing both ways. Even squares are round, after a fashion.

## 29/6/85

We were both surprised to see the wild irises, blooming in the ditch. What is the etymology of *bush*?

## 5/7/85

There is, tomorrow, a 40 percent chance of showers. Even the forecasters, here in the Interlake, resort to the mathematics of doubt. I listen to my cornflakes going soggy. Somewhere, behind the sound of outboard motors, a hawk is perched on a gopher's back.

## 6/7/85

Your skin, after our short nap, in this hot afternoon light, tastes like Paulin's Peerless Soda Crackers. Salted, of course. Yes, it was good for me too. I had no idea you once broke horses.

*You Are*
  *My Country & Western,*
*Lullaby*

## 11/7/85

Mr. Bad is a lady. I should have known that, I suppose. Guns are an aphrodisiac, if cowboy movies are what they seem. Last night you embraced me with all your arms. I made the mistake of counting.

## 12/7/85

West of Outlook, Saskatchewan, you can drive straight into the end of the world. There's a law against shade in that country. Trees are considered improper. Sometimes the cattle graze, for a whole week, in a mirage.

## 16/7/85

Another day of my life, washed down the gully. The camouflaged button cactus, for instance, is easily discovered by the bare foot. Barbed wire fences are not vegetarians. But then again, it's no skin off your ass, is it, love?

### 17/7/85

The hawk on the telephone pole, folding its wings like an angel at rest, is planning a gopher's visit to the blue sky. The grasshoppers hit our windshield like hail. You raise your head from my lap, asking what the sound is. This is called writing a landscape poem.

### 18/7/85

Cowboy's lament. Somebody stole my woman from me. She said his name was Mike. Or Ed. I forget which.

### 19/7/85

And *now* can I put on the potatoes? you say. But surely domestication is basic to the rise of civilization and the advance of the stock market. And do you mind if I take a short nap while the water boils?

### 20/7/85

We cherish our little sufferings, as humble as they might be. Last night it was chilly in my bedroom.

## 22/7/85

Does your mama know that you're going to hell?/
Does your mama know that you're doing it well?/
Does your mama know how you love to screw?/She
was pretty good in her day too,/they tell me.

## 25/7/85

When do you suppose time first began its unex-
pected return? The horizon is, apparently, a linguistic
illusion calculated to make us feel at once secure and
heroic. I am above all else happy when my tongue is
in your mouth.

## 29/7/85

The nearest shadow was four miles away. I had only
just begun that which, like falling in love, I cannot
control once commenced, when a Greyhound bus,
three half-tons, two galloping horses, a motorcycle
gang and a woman in a convertible began to con-
verge on the spot where I was standing with my
back to the road.

### 30/7/85

One assumes there is some reason (as yet undiscovered) for what is called propagation. These great flocks of birds, even now, practicing their migration, must be a sign. All that's missing is gin and tonic.

### 31/7/85

I know you'd be appalled at the idea of a faithful lover. I'll do my best

### 2/8/85

Premonitions are, I would imagine, a form of hindsight. My loathing for the human species is exceeded only by my need for human companionship. That survey crew you hired, to locate the absence of desire. Has it had any luck?

### 3/8/85

The hawk, at least at this distance, seems to soar without moving its wings. Do your lovers dislike being staked to the ground, naked, that way?

*The Dream*
  *of Leather*
*is Softly*
    *to Enfold*

## 11/8/85

I remember vividly the afternoon of my childhood when, in a violent downpour that included some hail, the sky rained frogs. A few of them croaked sweetly as they fell, filling the air with rigorous prophecy. They were quite right, I can't forget you.

## 12/8/85

Why do shoes dream? At night I hear them, under your bed, dreaming they will carry me away to mysterious places where I'll have to learn all over again how to walk, stepping first from a slippery rock ledge onto a wet log.

## 13/8/85

I would like to go much deeper into the heart of breaking. We should attempt one kiss, even if one only, inside the mouth of the crocodile.

### 15/8/85

Here on the bullheaded prairies we praise the sun with icicles. When summer betrays us, we recover in a regimen of parkas. One winter night, in a cold frenzy, I let my tongue freeze to an iron windmill. I knew then I was destined to be your lover.

### 18/8/85

Style is a way of thinking. Contemplate the rodeo rider, pitched wildly about by his fancy boots.

### 19/8/85

And my shirts. Do they grow tired of hanging, week after week, in a closet, just on the verge of slipping off their hangers and collapsing to the floor? Does the very possibility keep my shoes awake, listening, in the dark? Why didn't you call last night?

## 22/8/85

Apples, my father never once said in his life, are not avocados. How can a whip crack? Lust has its complement in hurricanes and plagues. Even the cankerworm, letting itself down from trees, is a nuisance only at the height of its cycle. What, exactly, are drumlins?

## 23/8/85

Stockings like yours aren't made for walking. The bathhouse by the sea, trala, is good enough, trala, for me. Or, as my father liked to remark, talk is cheap, whisky costs money.

## 25/8/85

The loop of the lariat takes the calf very nearly by surprise. I remember how, when I was a boy, the men, at cutting time, kept the knife clean in a raw potato. We would walk away gravely, each foot, finding itself left behind, hurrying to catch up and take the lead.

## 26/8/85

A goose egg, we used to call it, zero. Getting our kicks. But that was in school. We were learning. Later you would teach me naught.

## 28/8/85

Even elbows are easily bruised. Blood, like beer in a plastic cup at a picnic, comes in a fragile container. You say you like the glitter of spurs, raised to the shoulders of a bucking horse.

## 30/8/85

Water isn't afraid to fall. Wouldn't it be refreshing if, somewhere in the world, one rainbow, even if only for a moment, assumed the shape of an equilateral triangle?

## 31/8/85

You are a surgeon of mangos. Rhododendrons begin at home, while marigolds, given the opportunity, sport the kiss of an early frost.

You say that a full moon makes you hornier. If you'll pardon my grammarian's question, hornier than what? My flat-soled shoes imagine mountains.

*I Protect My*
    *Loneliness*
*the Way a Dog Protects*
    *the House*
        *of Its Dead Master*

21/9/85

Yes, I bought the tickets. I thought the sun had given up chuckwagon racing. We must get to bed early.


22/9/85

We are going to a place where things are only what they are. Or, with the barest exception, something else, but only just something else, hardly. Words are not allowed at all.


23/9/85

Dumplings are, you might say, a culinary exploration of the idea of realized chaos. I put the tickets in your purse, where you're certain not to find them.


24/9/85

The tower on the horizon was, it turns out, a beer can, dropped by someone from a speeding train. That would seem to be signally impossible, if is is at all what it is.

25/9/85

In Winnipeg the streets are skilfully designed to lead to railway tracks that can't be crossed. Poets, at the sight of an approaching train, place their poems on the tracks, hoping to have them pressed into pennies. Lovers crack sunflower seeds by placing the dried black faces of sunflowers under the wheels of locomotives that speak only to each other, from parallel roadbeds, late at night.

26/9/85

I bought two tickets, both of them for you. We are going to enter the imagination of flax. Now that winding the clock has been made unnecessary, even impossible, weavers are puzzled at how to shape their looms, and ghosts, especially those that wear black, cannot find the door of evening.

27/9/85

Words are like children skipping rope. We'll be sitting side by side.

## 28/9/85

I regret that I left the tickets in the top left drawer of the dresser you gave to The Salvation Army. The men who picked it up were wearing wings, which, at the time, struck me as inappropriate. In winter, in Winnipeg, the streets become maculate, iridescent, or, sometimes, imitating deserts which they no longer remember, clearly visionary.

## 29/9/85

Caribou, for instance, know how to paw with their hoofs through snow and find silken clumps of lichen. All the flights to Hawaii, from now until Ash Wednesday, are booked by polar bears. Don't forget to bring your guitar.

## 30/9/85

The streets of Winnipeg, in winter, become intentional. One learns to breathe cold iron. Testicles migrate, along with snow geese and other birds of questionable courage, to bayous and estuaries. Nipples eat frozen red berries off the mountain ash and various bushes. This is a prophecy.

Often, while performing, you wear a blossom on your skull, and the bees that come seeking make no sound.

I have the tickets here in my pocket. Why I pretended to have lost them, I can't imagine. Country singers and misanthropes get to sit on the clouds. You say you love me. This must be Indian summer.

*I Wanted*
*You*
*to Tell*
*Me*

### 14/10/85

You are the question to all my answers. I was an echo without prior sound until you, silently, wrote, "I am counting on my fingers to remember you." If only you had got my name right.

### 17/10/85

Turn about is fur play. "Almost daily," you add, "I check the garden." But please, love, no fall plowing with frost in the ground. The plowshare, too, has its fear of the dark.

### 18/10/85

Hearing day break, we pillow our heads. I want to explain. The buffalo was only there in my mind, apparently. You had forgot to set the alarm.

## 20/10/85

What I remember tonight is my mother at the kitchen table, cleaning eggs. The crate was not quite full. She sent me out to the barn to find one more egg. It was there, that afternoon, climbing the steps to the hayloft, I fell into the chasm between disbelief and longing.

## 1/11/85

The guitar plays itself on your fingers. I hear the seeds of the dandelion, torn into the air by your breath. Or is it snow I see, at the entrance to your mouth?

## 4/11/85

Pickerel cheeks and saskatoon pie. Those delicacies give to Lake Winnipeg at once a refulgence and a pungency. Love has its brightness too, that only the tongue can smell.

5/11/85

"When we run out of places to touch," you reminded me, "we resort to tasting." We were eating scallops. You said you have your grandmother's mouth. It was nearly midnight.


8/11/85

Don't strike a match on a rainbow. But why not?


9/11/85

There are, of course, brown cows that we refer to as red. Try putting a flame into a wooden crate marked This Side Up.


13/11/85

Years ago, playing in my bare feet on a pile of discarded lumber, I stepped on a nail. What I can't forget is not the surprise of entry but, rather, the extraction, the red-pepper grip of muscle and bone, the vacuum screaming its pain.

*Even After We Came
    the Snow Was Still
There, on the Roofs,
    Crying
        in the Moonlight*

Clocks are not cuckoos, though I'm not quite certain what a cuckoo is. Comparisons are of limited
use, it would seem. Your eyes, I'm told, are like
precious stones. And you wonder why I'm posses-
sive.

We learn to stop caring by painting the black cow
white. Every passion has its color. Why are your
eyes one green, one blue? I see that you strum your
guitar until your fingers begin to bleed, then you
add love to your repertoire.

"Today I thought I saw a butterfly on a planter
topped with snow." This, in your note, the one you
left on the fridge, when you didn't drive me to the
airport.

## 25/11/85

I arrived in Baghdad intending to drink yogurt and to eat fresh dates. Even as we landed a voice on the loudspeaker system observed, obscurely, "We are going down." My silence was the color of your pubic invitation.

## 26/11/85

Arabic wisdom. "The truth is too precious to share." And so our hands grope in the dark, finding buckles and zippers. We say nothing.

## 27/11/85

I think of ziggurats, their lifted entrances, their lost stairways. They knew everything in advance. I had no idea the desert, from the sky, would appear so close in color to red.

## 28/11/85

Your nipples are as a pair, twinned kumquats, brazen in the sun. But is it true they turn away, avoiding each other's light, under the crazed umbrella of my body?

**29/11/85**

The festive ululations of the women, their tongues quick in the red openness of their mouths, their voices high into ecstasy, drove me to the bliss of ruin. I stayed in the desert forever.

**30/11/85**

"We live," she said, "a whole life with the same person. It makes us very old." I sipped my coffee. From far in the distance, I heard artillery. "Then you are not," I said, "Ishtar." She wore a dozen bracelets on each of her golden arms. "You have known her for a long time," she told me.

**1/12/85**

The bazaar is full of men who are pounding tin and copper into the roundness of your buttocks. The din of their brassy fever brought a stout handle to my hand. I watched a man turning the rim of a pan on his big toe. You poured me, softly.

## 2/12/85

In the dust, by the Euphrates, I put my mouth to your bum. It was right there, in bas-relief, on a brick wall the color of sand, in the ancient sunlight. The river flows in a curve around what was once Babylon.

## 3/12/85

The gate is off its hinges. But I love you just the slam. And the proof of the pudding, Ishtar, is. I am mad today, with missing you. You are everywhere.

## 4/12/85

The date palms shape the landscape. There are two hundred varieties. Or more. Or less. How then can I call anything love, unless it is as various as you, deciduous? But leaf me be.

## 7/12/85

I remember clearly now. I went down onto my knees. You put your hand to the back of my neck. The water buffalo, grazing at the edge of the river, lifting its head to your long moan, looked vaguely like a unicorn.

Even the two ends of an egg have difficulty under-
standing each other. As a child I believed that rabbits
lay eggs, and in that knowledge I was complete.